"IF"

Love through me, Love of God,
  Make me like Thy clear air
Through which unhindered, colours pass
  As though it were not there.

Powers of the love of God,
  Depths of the heart Divine,
O Love that faileth not, break forth,
  And flood this world of Thine.

The cover illustration is of the Via Dolorosa, along which our Lord is traditionally held to have walked on His way to Calvary.

"IF"

Amy Carmichael

A Dohnavur Book

LONDON

SPCK

First published 1938
Twentieth impression 1978

SPCK
Holy Trinity Church
Marylebone Road
London NW1 4DU

Printed in Great Britain by
Fletcher & Son Ltd, Norwich

ISBN 0 281 00394 7

HOW "IF" CAME TO BE WRITTEN

ONE evening a fellow-worker brought me a trouble about a younger one who was missing the way of Love. This led to a wakeful night, for the word at such times is always, "Lord, is it I? Have I failed her anywhere? What do I know of Calvary Love?" And then sentence by sentence the "Ifs" came, almost as if spoken aloud to the inward ear.

Next morning they were shared with another (for they had been written down in pencil in the night), and then a few others shared. After this some copies were printed on our little hand-press for the D.F. only; and that led to this booklet.

At first when it was asked for, we felt, No, it is far too private for that. But if it can help any to understand what the life of love means and to live that life, then it is not ours to refuse.

Some of the "Ifs" appear to be related to pride, selfishness, or cowardice, but digging deeper we come upon an unsuspected lovelessness at the root of them all. *The pages in Part 2 are not meant to be read one after the other.* Perhaps only one here and there may have the needed word, and leaving the others, the reader may find something in the last pages.

And in case any true follower be troubled by the "*then I know nothing,*" I would say, the thought came in this form, and I fear to weaken it. But here, as everywhere, the letter killeth. St. Paul counted the loss of all things as nothing that he might know Him whom he already knew ; and the soul, suddenly illuminated by some fresh outshining of the knowledge of the love of God shown forth on Calvary, does not stop to measure how much or how little it knew of that love before. Penetrated, melted, broken before that vision of love, it feels that indeed all it ever knew was nothing, less than nothing.

It is clear, I think, that such a booklet

as this is not meant for every one, but only for those who are called to be under-shepherds. And there are some of them for whom it has no word. They have already entered into that of which I have been impelled to write.

A. C.

PART I

There are times when something comes into our lives which is charged with love in such a way that it seems to open the Eternal to us for a moment, or at least some of the Eternal Things, and the greatest of these is love.

It may be a small and intimate touch upon us or our affairs, light as the touch of the dawn-wind on the leaves of the tree, something not to be captured and told to another in words. But we know that it is our Lord. And then perhaps the room where we are, with its furniture and books and flowers, seems less "present" than His Presence, and the heart is drawn into that sweetness of which the old hymn sings.

The love of Jesus what it is
None but His loved ones know.

Or it is the dear human love about us that bathes us as in summer seas and rests us through and through. Can we ever cease to wonder at the love of our companions? And then suddenly we recognise our Lord in them. It is His love that they lavish upon us. O Love of God made manifest in Thy lovers, we worship Thee.

Or (not often, perhaps, for dimness seems to be more wholesome for us here, but sometimes, because our Lord is very merciful) it is given to us to look up through the blue air and see the love of God. And yet, after all, how little we see! "*That ye may be able to comprehend what is the breadth and length and depth and height and to know the love of Christ which passeth knowledge*"—the words are too great for us. What do we comprehend, what do we know? Confounded and abased, we enter into the Rock and hide

2

us in the dust before the glory of the Majesty of love—the love whose symbol is the Cross.

And a question pierces then : What do I know of Calvary love ?

PART II

If I have not compassion on my fellow-servant even as my Lord had pity on me, then I know nothing of Calvary love.

If I belittle those whom I am called to serve, talk of their weak points in contrast perhaps with what I think of as my strong points ; if I adopt a superior attitude, forgetting "Who made thee to differ ? and what hast thou that thou hast not received ? " then I know nothing of Calvary love.

If I can easily discuss the shortcomings and the sins of any; if I can speak in a casual way even of a child's misdoings, then I know nothing of Calvary love.

If I find myself half-carelessly taking lapses for granted, " Oh, that's what they always do," " Oh, of course she talks like that, he acts like that," then I know nothing of Calvary love.

If I can enjoy a joke at the expense of another; if I can in any way slight another in conversation, or even in thought, then I know nothing of Calvary love.

If I can write an unkind letter, speak an unkind word, think an unkind thought without grief and shame, then I know nothing of Calvary love.

If I do not feel far more for the grieved Saviour than for my worried self when troublesome things occur, then I know nothing of Calvary love.

If I know little of His pitifulness (*the Lord turned and looked upon Peter*), if I know little of His courage of hopefulness for the truly humble and penitent (He saith unto him, Feed My lambs), then I know nothing of Calvary love.

If I deal with wrong for any other reason than that implied in the words, *"From His right hand went a fiery law for them. Yea, He loved the people;"* if I can rebuke without a pang, then I know nothing of Calvary love.

If, in dealing with one who does not respond, I weary of the strain, and slip from under the burden, then I know nothing of Calvary love.

If I cannot bear to be like the father who did not soften the rigours of the far country ; if, in this sense, I refuse to allow the law of God (the way of transgressors is hard) to take effect, because of the distress it causes me to see that law in operation, then I know nothing of Calvary love.

If I am perturbed by the reproach and misunderstanding that may follow action taken for the good of souls for whom I must give account; if I cannot commit the matter and go on in peace and in silence, remembering Gethsemane and the Cross, then I know nothing of Calvary love.

If I cannot catch " the sound of noise of rain " * long before the rain falls, and, going to some hilltop of the spirit, as near to my God as I can, have not faith to wait there with my face between my knees, though six times or sixty times I am told " there is nothing," till at last " there arises a little cloud out of the sea," then I know nothing of Calvary love.

* 1 Kings 18. 41 margin.

If my attitude be one of fear, not faith, about one who has disappointed me, if I say, "Just what I expected," if a fall occurs, then I know nothing of Calvary love.

If I do not look with eyes of hope on all in whom there is even a faint beginning, as our Lord did, when, just after His disciples had wrangled about which of them should be accounted the greatest, He softened His rebuke with those heart-melting words, " *Ye are they which have continued with Me in My temptations,*" then I know nothing of Calvary love.

If I cast up a confessed, repented and forsaken sin against another, and allow my remembrance of that sin to colour my thinking and feed my suspicions, then I know nothing of Calvary love.

If I have not the patience of my Saviour with souls who grow slowly ; if I know little of travail (a sharp and painful thing) till Christ be fully formed in them, then I know nothing of Calvary love.

If I sympathise weakly with weakness, and say to one who is turning back from the Cross, Pity thyself ; if I refuse such a one the sympathy that braces and the brave and heartening word of comradeship, then I know nothing of Calvary love.

If I cannot keep silence over a disappointing soul (unless for the sake of that soul's good or for the good of others it be necessary to speak), then I know nothing of Calvary love.

If I can hurt another by speaking faithfully without much preparation of spirit, and without hurting myself far more than I hurt that other, then I know nothing of Calvary love.

If I am afraid to speak the truth, lest I lose affection, or lest the one concerned should say, "You do not understand," or because I fear to lose my reputation for kindness; if I put my own good name before the other's highest good, then I know nothing of Calvary love.

If I am content to heal a hurt slightly, saying Peace, peace, where is no peace; if I forget the poignant word " Let love be without dissimulation " and blunt the edge of truth, speaking not right things but smooth things, then I know nothing of Calvary love.

If I fear to hold another to the highest because it is so much easier to avoid doing so, then I know nothing of Calvary love.

If I hold on to choices of any kind, just because they are my choice ; if I give any room to my private likes and dislikes, then I know nothing of Calvary love.

If I put my own happiness before the well-being of the work entrusted to me ; if, though I have this ministry and have received much mercy, I faint, then I know nothing of Calvary love.

If I am soft to myself and slide comfortably into the vice of self-pity and self-sympathy ; if I do not by the grace of God practise fortitude, then I know nothing of Calvary love.

If I myself dominate myself, if my thoughts revolve round myself, if I am so occupied with myself I rarely have " a heart at leisure from itself," then I know nothing of Calvary love.

If, the moment I am conscious of the shadow of self crossing my threshold, I do not shut the door, and in the power of Him who works in us to will and to do, keep that door shut, then I know nothing of Calvary love.

If I cannot in honest happiness take the second place (or the twentieth); if I cannot take the first without making a fuss about my unworthiness, then I know nothing of Calvary love.

If, when I am able to discover something which has baffled others, I forget Him who revealeth the deep and secret things, and knoweth what is in the darkness and showeth it to us ; if I forget that it was He who granted that ray of light to His most unworthy servant, then I know nothing of Calvary love.

If I cannot be at rest under the Unexplained, forgetting the word, *And blessed is he whosoever shall not be offended in Me*; or if I can admit the least shadow of a misunderstanding, then I know nothing of Calvary love.

If I do not give a friend " the benefit of the doubt," but put the worst construction instead of the best on what is said or done, then I know nothing of Calvary love.

If I take offence easily, if I am content to continue in a cool unfriendliness, though friendship be possible, then I know nothing of Calvary love.

If a sudden jar can cause me to speak an impatient, unloving word, then I know nothing of Calvary love.*

* For a cup brimful of sweet water cannot spill even one drop of bitter water however suddenly jolted.

If I feel injured when another lays to my charge things that I know not, forgetting that my Sinless Saviour trod this path to the end, then I know nothing of Calvary love.

If I feel bitterly towards those who condemn me, as it seems to me, unjustly, forgetting that if they knew me as I know myself they would condemn me much more, then I know nothing of Calvary love.

If I say, "Yes, I forgive, but I cannot forget," as though the God, who twice a day washes all the sands on all the shores of all the world, could not wash such memories from my mind, then I know nothing of Calvary love.

If one whose help I greatly need appears to be as content to build in wood, hay, stubble, as in gold, silver, precious stones, and I hesitate to obey my light and do without that help because so few will understand, then I know nothing of Calvary love.

If the care of a soul (or a community) be entrusted to me, and I consent to subject it to weakening influences, because the voice of the world—my immediate Christian world—fills my ears, then I know nothing of Calvary love.

If by doing some work which the undiscerning consider " not spiritual work " I can best help others, and I inwardly rebel, thinking it is the spiritual for which I crave, when in truth it is the interesting and exciting, then I know nothing of Calvary love.

If monotony tries me, and I cannot stand drudgery ; if stupid people fret me and little ruffles set me on edge ; if I make much of the trifles of life, then I know nothing of Calvary love.

If I am inconsiderate about the comfort of others, or their feelings, or even of their little weaknesses ; if I am careless about their little hurts and miss opportunities to smooth their way ; if I make the sweet running of household wheels more difficult to accomplish, then I know nothing of Calvary love.

If interruptions annoy me, and private cares make me impatient ; if I shadow the souls about me because I myself am shadowed, then I know nothing of Calvary love.

If souls can suffer alongside, and I hardly know it, because the spirit of discernment is not in me, then I know nothing of Calvary love.

If there be any reserve in my giving to Him who so loved that He gave His Dearest for me ; if there be a secret " but " in my prayer, " anything but that, Lord," then I know nothing of Calvary love.

If I become entangled in any " inordinate affection; " if things or places or people hold me back from obedience to my Lord, then I know nothing of Calvary love.

If something I am asked to do for another feels burdensome ; if, yielding to an inward unwillingness, I avoid doing it, then I know nothing of Calvary love.

If the praise of man elates me and his blame depresses me ; if I cannot rest under misunderstanding without defending myself ; if I love to be loved more than to love, to be served more than to serve, then I know nothing of Calvary love.

If I crave hungrily to be used to show the way of liberty to a soul in bondage, instead of caring only that it be delivered ; if I nurse my disappointment when I fail, instead of asking that to another the word of release may be given, then I know nothing of Calvary love.

If I want to be known as the doer of something that has proved the right thing, or as the one who suggested that it should be done, then I know nothing of Calvary love.

If I do not forget about such a trifle as personal success, so that it never crosses my mind, or if it does, is never given a moment's room there ; if the cup of spiritual flattery tastes sweet to me, then I know nothing of Calvary love.

If it be not a simple and a natural thing to say, "Enviest thou for my sake? would God that all the Lord's people were prophets," then I know nothing of Calvary love.

If in the fellowship of service I seek to attach a friend to myself, so that others are caused to feel unwanted; if my friendships do not draw others deeper in, but are ungenerous (to myself, for myself), then I know nothing of Calvary love.

If I refuse to allow one who is dear to me to suffer for the sake of Christ, if I do not see such suffering as the greatest honour that can be offered to any follower of the Crucified, then I know nothing of Calvary love.

If I slip into the place that can be filled by Christ alone, making myself the first necessity to a soul instead of leading it to fasten upon Him, then I know nothing of Calvary love.

If my interest in the work of others is cool; if I think in terms of my own special work; if the burdens of others are not my burdens too, and their joys mine, then I know nothing of Calvary love.

If, when an answer I did not expect comes to a prayer which I believed I truly meant, I shrink back from it ; if the burden my Lord asks me to bear be not the burden of my heart's choice, and I fret inwardly and do not welcome His will, then I know nothing of Calvary love.

If I avoid being "ploughed under," with all that such ploughing entails of rough handling, isolation, uncongenial situations, strange tests, then I know nothing of Calvary love.

If I wonder why something trying is allowed, and press for prayer that it may be removed ; if I cannot be trusted with any disappointment, and cannot go on in peace under any mystery, then I know nothing of Calvary love.

If I make much of anything appointed, magnify it secretly to myself or insidiously to others ; if I let them think it " hard," if I look back longingly upon what used to be, and linger among the bye-ways of memory, so that my power to help is weakened, then I know nothing of Calvary love.

If the love that " alone maketh light of every heavy thing, and beareth evenly every uneven thing " is not my heart's desire, then I know nothing of Calvary love.

If I refuse to be a corn of wheat that falls into the ground and dies (" is separated from all in which it lived before "), then I know nothing of Calvary love.

If I ask to be delivered from trial rather than for deliverance out of it, to the praise of His glory; if I forget that the way of the Cross leads to the Cross and not to a bank of flowers; if I regulate my life on these lines, or even unconsciously my thinking, so that I am surprised when the way is rough and think it strange, though the word is, *Think it not strange, Count it all joy*, then I know nothing of Calvary love.

If the ultimate, the hardest, cannot be asked of me ; if my fellows hesitate to ask it and turn to someone else, then I know nothing of Calvary love.

If I covet any place on earth but the dust at the foot of the Cross, then I know nothing of Calvary love.

That which I know not, teach Thou me,
O Lord, my God.

PART III

I have felt these words scorching to write, but it is borne upon me, that in spite of all our hymns and prayers (so many of them for love), it is possible to be content with the shallows of love, if indeed such shallows should be called love at all.

(Perhaps prayer often needs to be followed by a little pause, that we may have time to open our hearts to that for which we have prayed. We often rush from prayer to prayer without waiting for the word within, which says, "I have heard you, My child.")

The more we ponder our Lord's words about love, and the burning words the Spirit gave to His followers to write, the more acutely do we feel our deadly lack. The Search-light of the Spirit discovers us to ourselves, and such a discovery leaves us appalled. How can even He who is the God of all patience have patience with us ? Like Job we abhor ourselves and repent in dust and ashes.

But the light is not turned upon us to rob us of our hope. There is a lifting up. If only we desire to be purged from self with its entangling nets, its subtleties, its disguises (false-hoods truly) its facile showing of brass for gold, as the Tamil says ; if, hating unlove from the ground of the heart, we cry to be delivered, then our God will be to us a God of deliverances.

2

No vision of the night can show, no word declare with what longings of love Divine Love waits till the heart, all weary

F

and sick of itself, turns to its Lord and says, "Take full possession." There is no need to plead that the love of God shall fill our heart as though He were unwilling to fill us : He is willing as light is willing to flood a room that is opened to its brightness ; willing as water is willing to flow into an emptied channel. Love is pressing round us on all sides like air. Cease to resist, and instantly love takes possession. As the 15th century poem *Quia amore langues* says,

> *Long and love thou never so high,*
> *My love is more than thine may be.*

More, far more. For as His abundance of pardon passes our power to tell it, so does His abundance of love : it is far as the East is from the West, high as the heaven is above the earth. But words fail : Love soars above them all.

To look at ourselves leads to despair.
Thank God, the Blood cleanseth.

If thou be foul, I shall make thee clean,
If thou be sick, I shall thee heal.
Foundest thou ever love so leal?

Never, Lord, never.

3

Sometimes, when we are distressed by past failure and tormented by fear of failure in the future should we again set our faces toward Jerusalem, nothing helps so much as to give some familiar Scripture time to enter into us and become part of our being. The words " Grace for grace " have been a help to me since I read in a little old book of Bishop Moule's something that opened their meaning. (Till then I had not understood them.)

He says " for " means simply *instead*, " The image is of a perpetual succession

73

of supply; a displacement ever going on; ceaseless changes of need and demand.

"The picture before us is as of a river. Stand on its banks, and contemplate the flow of waters. A minute passes, and another. Is it the same stream still? Yes. But is it the same water? No. The liquid mass that passed you a few seconds ago fills now another section of the channel ; new water has displaced it, or if you please replaced it; *water instead of water*. And so hour by hour, and year by year, and century by century, the process holds ; one stream, other waters, living not stagnant, because always in the great identity there is perpetual exchange. Grace takes the place of grace ; " (Love takes the place of love) " ever new, ever old, ever the same, ever fresh and young, for hour by hour, for year by year, through Christ."

4

There is no force strong enough to hold us together as a company, and animate all our doings, but this one force of Love; and so there is a constant attack upon the love without which we are sounding brass and tinkling cymbal.

That explains why every now and then those who want to live the life of love seem to be constrained to seek the searching and the cleansing of the Spirit of God, first (it has often happened so) in the secret of our own hearts, and then together; and we know how graciously God has answered us, so that though our word must always be, "not as though I had already attained," we do, by His enabling, press onward.

There is another reason why the adversary attacks love. It is this :—

Far out on our uttermost rim a thing may occur which is the reflection, so to speak, of something that was nourished in the heart of one who is in the very centre. I have often known it to be so. Perhaps it was never expressed in act or word, the eye did not see it, the ear did not hear it. But spiritual influences move where sight and hearing have no place; and unlove in any one of us, or even an absence of the quality of love of which we have been thinking, is enough to cause the slow stain to spread till it reaches some soul in a moment of its weakness. And irreparable harm may result.

O Lord, forgive : Thy property is always to have mercy. Give me the comfort of Thy help again. Let it be Thy pleasure to deliver me, O Lord my God.

*   *   *

5

The way of love is never an easy way. If our hearts be set on walking in that way we must be prepared to suffer. "It was the way the Master went; should not the servant tread it still?" It is possible that we may be enclosed in circumstances which drain natural love, till we feel dry as grass on an Indian hillside under a burning sun.

We have toiled for some one dear to us, but never knew it toil. We have poured out stores of health never to be recovered, but did not know it, nor would we have cared if we had known it, so dearly did we love. And all our hope was that the one so cherished would become a minister to others. But it was not so.

And then unwillingly we become aware of a strange unresponsiveness in the one for whom nothing had seemed too much to do, a coldness that chilled, a hardness that pushed away as with hard hands the heart that had almost broken to save that life from destruction.

Then (but only those who have gone

through such a bereft hour will understand)
a fear worse than any pain has us in its
grip : is the love of the years slipping
from us ? " Father, forgive them, for they
know not what they do "—is that fading
from our memory ? Love never faileth,
is love failing now ? Shall we find ourselves meeting lovelessness with lovelessness ?

In such an hour, a prayer now many
years old, that felt a desperate prayer,
burned into words :

> *Deep unto deep, O Lord,*
> *Crieth in me,*
> *Gathering strength I come,*
> *Lord, unto Thee.*
> *Jesus of Calvary,*
> *Smitten for me,*
> *Ask what Thou wilt, but give*
> *Love to me.*

Yes, ask what Thou wilt, any hopes, any

joys of human affection, any rewards of love, but let not love depart. Nothing ordinary is equal to this new call; nothing in me suffices for this. O Lord of Love and Lord of Pain, abound in me in love : Love through me, Love of God.

6

Our dear Lord listens to the prayer that goeth not out of feigned lips, and it is written for our comfort that He causes those who love Him to inherit substance, the wonderful '' substance '' that is grace instead of grace, the perpetual gift of His Fulness. This grace is no mere '' impersonal substance,'' but God working in us, the Lord in action in our very springs of thought and will. God is Love, so, for us, Love is this blessed '' Substance '' that the children of the Father are caused to inherit.

It is the river's word again. The empty

river-bed " inherits " the water that pours through it from the heights, it does not create that water, it only receives it, and its treasuries are filled, its pools overflow for the blessing and refreshment of the land. It is so with us ; our treasuries of time, our years with all their months, weeks, days, hours, minutes, are filled with the flowing treasure of love that we may help others. Who could have thought of such joy for us but He whose name is Love? Now unto Him that is able to do exceeding abundantly above all that we ask or think, according to the power that worketh in us, unto Him be glory.

7

Let us end on a very simple note : Let us listen to simple words ; our Lord speaks simply : " Trust Me, My child," He says. " Trust Me with a humbler heart and a fuller abandon to My will than ever thou didst before. Trust Me to pour My love through thee, as minute succeeds minute. And if thou shouldst be conscious of anything hindering the flow, do not hurt My love by going away from Me in discouragement, nothing can hurt love so much as that. Draw all the closer to Me, come, flee unto Me to hide thee, even from thyself. Tell Me about the trouble. Trust Me to turn My hand upon thee and throughly to remove the boulder that has choked thy river-bed, and take away all the sand that has silted up the channel. I will not leave thee until I have done that which I have spoken to thee of. I will perfect that which concerneth thee. Fear thou not, O child of My love ; fear not."

*   *   *

And now to gather all in one page :—

Beloved, let us love.
Lord, what is love ?

Love is that which inspired My life, and led Me to My Cross, and held Me on My Cross. Love is that which will make it thy joy to lay down thy life for thy brethren.

Lord, evermore give me this love.

Blessed are they which do hunger and thirst after love, for they shall be filled.

DOHNAVUR BOOKS
by Amy Carmichael
Published by SPCK

STORIES OF INDIAN WOMEN
Ponnammal (paper)
Mimosa (paper)

DEVOTIONAL BOOKS
His Thoughts Said . . . His Father Said . . .
(paper)
Edges of His Ways (paper)
If (paper)
God's Missionary (paper)
Gold by Moonlight (cloth)

BOOK OF VERSE
Toward Jerusalem (paper)

THE DOHNAVUR FELLOWSHIP

ORIGIN. The work in Dohnavur, South India, began in 1901, when Amy Carmichael, while doing itinerant evangelistic work, came to know that little girls were sometimes taken and trained as dancing-girls for the Hindu temples—which meant a life of evil for them. Wherever she could, she saved children from this fate, and, with her as "Mother", the Family in Dohnavur began.

In recent years good laws have been passed, and the dedication of girls to temples made illegal. Danger still exists, however, though its sources are changing and hard to trace. In spite of legislation, and both Government and private efforts, houses of ill-fame seem to be on the increase, and it is known that little girls are brought up in some of these, even from babyhood, with immoral purposes in view. Boys are also in moral danger. We make a home for any baby or older child whom we have reason to think may otherwise fall into the hands of those who would so train and use it.

OBJECTIVE. The deliverance of these children, their spiritual salvation and their training to serve others are our main objectives. Sometimes we are able to shelter older girls and women. We seek to succour the desolate and suffering, and to make the love of

God and His plan of redemption in its fulness known to all whom we can reach.

WORK AND WORKERS. We are a company of people, both Indian and from overseas, men and women, married and single, whose common loyalty is to our Lord and Saviour, Jesus Christ. This binds us to one another. We have many children and young people under our care: babies, toddlers, and younger schoolboys and schoolgirls in Dohnavur, while older boys and girls, and young men and women, are receiving education and training in various institutions all over the Madras State (and even farther afield). The latter are based either on Dohnavur or on one of our out-stations. In some cases the out-station is itself a training centre. The need of shepherding them all continues till they are securely launched in life elsewhere, or have become our fellow-workers here. Some who are ill-adjusted spiritually may be a care and a problem for years, and the handicapped naturally become a permanent part of the Family.

Our Hospital provides treatment for the people of the countryside as well as for those of the Family who may be ill. From time to time we have established temporary medical outposts. The majority of the staff have grown up in our own Family.

Although we come from various denominations, we are all evangelical. We do not belong officially to any of the organized churches, but seek to serve all in our neighbourhood, and calls for help sometimes come from further afield also.

ADMINISTRATION AND FINANCE. The headquarters of the work is in Dohnavur, and we have no controlling body elsewhere. We have an Office in London, and friends in other lands act as Honorary Secretaries.

Our Heavenly Father has promised to supply all our needs according to His riches in glory by Christ Jesus. We make no appeal for funds, and do not authorize anyone to make such appeals. We have found it enough to look to Him to direct us in all things, to overcome every difficulty, and to provide for every need.

ADDRESSES

The Dohnavur Fellowship, Dohnavur, Tirunelveli District, Tamil Nadu 627102, South India.
The Dohnavur Fellowship, 33 Church Road, Wimbledon, London, SW19 5DQ.

Dohnavur, 1978